# What God Really Wants?

by
**Durie Burns**

Copyright © 2012 by Durie Burns.

ALL RIGHTS RESERVED

The text of this publication, or any part thereof, may not be reproduced or transmitted in any form or by any means, electronic or mechanical, including photocopying, recording, storage in an information-retrieval system, or otherwise, without the prior written permission of the author. To request permission, please contact Durie Burns at (716) 818-0110 or e-mail him at durieb@yahoo.com.

Edited by Anthony Ambrogio

Cover Design by Brittany Jackson

Published by G Publishing LLC

Library of Congress Control Number: 2012941243

ISBN: 978-0-9849360-6-9

Printed in the United States of America

# Dedication

This book is dedicated to Reverend Whitfield Washington, Jr. You were in many ways a great influence in my life, and you never knew it. May you rest in peace.

# Acknowledgements

Thank you to all the people throughout my lifetime who gave me their opinions of what God really wants. If not for you, this book would not exist.

To all the people who encouraged me throughout the writing and publishing process of this book, you hold a special place in my heart.

To my friend Shirley in Saskatoon, Canada, I will always cherish the input and conversations we have had regarding this book. Your inspiration is one of the main reasons I decided to publish it.

Finally, I want to give special thanks to the person to whom this book is dedicated, the Rev. Whitfield Washington, Jr.

# Table of Contents

Prelude .................................................................. 1
Chapter 1 – Why ..................................................... 4
Chapter 2 – Religious Man ..................................... 7
Chapter 3 – Black People & Religion .................... 10
Chapter 4 – Whom to Follow ................................. 13
Chapter 5 – The Jesus Business ............................. 19
Chapter 6 – The Catholic Church and Wealth ....... 30
Chapter 7 – Religious Leaders and Crime ............. 37
Chapter 8 – War and Religion ................................ 44
Chapter 9 – God and Gay People ........................... 50
Chapter 10 – Stop the Madness .............................. 57
Chapter 11 – God's Blessings ................................. 59
Chapter 12 – Mega Churches ................................. 62
Chapter 13 – Religion and Politics ......................... 66
Chapter 14 – Religion and Racism ......................... 71
Chapter 15 – It's up to Us ....................................... 73
Chapter 16 – Free Will ............................................ 80
Chapter 17 – My Dream ......................................... 84
About the Author .................................................... 87

# Prelude

*I want everyone who might read this book to understand that it reflects my thinking and is not necessarily a factual assessment of religion and/or the Bible.* This book lays out my opinions, backed up by some facts, about topics that I have discussed with Christians and other religious people, including many religious leaders, over the years.

I was raised a Baptist and attended church regularly until I was a seventeen-year-old freshman at a Presbyterian college in Charlotte, North Carolina. Religion filled my life up to that point, when I began to wonder why so many people believed the Bible.

Over the years, I have had relatives, friends, and even strangers try to force their views of their religion on me, and I am so sick and tired of it. I have a problem with the hypocrisy: people tell me how I should live, but do not live that way themselves. And I am also troubled that religious people seem to justify anything they do, right or wrong, by reciting passages in the Bible. They cite them as if they are certain that what the passages say is the truth.

I just wish people would think twice instead of blindly believing and thus becoming unsuspecting participants in the biggest farce ever bestowed upon humanity. I am not saying that believing in God is a farce. Believing blindly in religion and religious leaders, however, *is* a farce. What makes people think that religious leaders are to be trusted unequivocally? Many religious leaders are not true Men or Women of God.

This is not the first book to question religious leaders and their messages about what God wants from us and for us. That's because I am not the first to know that everyone should question the pronouncements of religious leaders when it comes to interpreting the Bible and dictating how God wants us to live. The people I have met whom I consider true Men of God have no problem with being questioned about their religion because they are mostly living the life God wants his leaders and people to live.

For years, I refused to believe in God because I saw so many religious leaders and Christians living the same life I was living, yet telling me I was wrong for not believing the way they believed. I myself would never claim to be a Man of God unless I decided to live the way I believe God wants us to live. So I decided to write this book to let readers experience and understand the confusion in my words; brought on by what I believe were lies religious leaders and other religious minded-people tried to ingrain in me.

I want you to understand that I believe there may be a God but that he did not intend for us to force him on anyone. I believe God's plan for us is simple and unrelenting—that he wants us to do for others if we want a place with him. I believe those people who do things only for themselves and deceive others will pay when they meet God; and the decision between heaven and hell arrives.

# Chapter 1 – Why

***When the thought to write this book first came to mind, I was very surprised.*** I could not understand why I would even consider writing a book about God. I have wrestled with the idea of this book for a long time. In fact, I still hesitate to finish it. I finally decided to continue writing it as therapy for myself. I needed to say what kept coming to mind. That way, maybe I could finally stop thinking about it. It has become an unwanted burden, and I cannot explain why. However, the book is and will continue to be an ongoing project as I find issues I think people need to hear.

It has taken me a long time to write this book for a number of reasons. As you read it, you might be able to understand my hesitation. Initially, I never intended to publish it. In fact, on numerous occasions, I stopped writing. I felt reluctant, in part, because of my concerns about publishing it. My original plan was to write it and share it with my family and a few friends for their thoughts on the subject.

However, over these past few years, some people have pushed me to continue writing and to get it

*What God Really Wants*

published because they say people need to hear what I have to say. They say the world needs to know my thoughts. However, unlike them, I am not sure my words will convince anyone that my thoughts are inspired.

I hope what I write, if it is published, will influence people to trust their hearts and believe that God is a forgiving and merciful God, not a vengeful or violent God. Whatever happens, I know I just want to get the words out because I believe I am being compelled to do so.

If published, I vow that any money generated from its sale, except for a relatively small stipend, will go towards my dream of building apartment homes for homeless people who are in their situation not by choice. For example; people who lost their jobs because of corporate downsizing or job exportation, ex-military personnel, and/or men, women, and children who need a safe place from abusive spouses, parents, or others, not to mention those men and women who need a second chance in life because of a costly mistake they made and truly regret. You know the people of whom I speak. They're the ones the "Good Christians" refuse to hire (while at the same time these "Christians" tell us how God says to forgive).

This is just the beginning of my dream. My dream goes deeper than you can imagine. In my dream, I see a world where all people are respected; where

Durie Burns

people with the means voluntarily share with those in need. Where there are no homeless, no orphans, no poor, no hungry, no one in need or want. Where leaders of all countries learn to share their land; where war is not an option and people remember to share the assets that God put on this Earth for us all. For I believe, this is what God really wants.

# Chapter 2 – Religious Man

***I am not religious in the way most religious people would describe a religious man.*** As I stated earlier, I was raised a Baptist. When I was in my teens, some people even thought I might someday become a minister.

Instead, I followed a different path. As I grew older, I began to question the Bible and the things people said about the events that allegedly occurred in it. I say "allegedly" because nobody alive today can actually verify their truth. However, when you speak to believers, they adamantly state they know that everything in the Bible is true. When I ask them how they know, they tell me because the Bible says it is so.

When I ask religious people if God wrote the Bible, they tell me that people whom God influenced wrote the passages. These religious people will be some of the same individuals who will denounce this book as the work of a person who knows absolutely nothing about the Bible or God. They may say I am crazy and do not know what I am talking about. Some may even call me a lunatic or the devil himself.

Durie Burns

However, if you can believe that the passages in the Bible were divinely inspired, how do you know that what I am writing is not? After all, no one alive today, including me, really knows whether my words are inspired or not, just like the words in the Bible.

To those who will say I know nothing about the Bible, I say to you that religious people have instructed me about the Bible throughout my lifetime. In addition, I have read the book myself – parts of some chapters and all of some others.

Most of the church followers I have spoken with have not read the Bible any more than I have. They, as I did when I was young, depended on their religious leaders to interpret it for them. What they were told became the truth for them. Why? Because a person they respected said it was so.

Even Biblical scholars differ about the true story of Jesus, the resurrection, and other parts of the Bible as it is written. In April 2007, a news story revealed that Jesus' last supper did not take place in the place where the Bible says it did. In addition, the story indicated that there were female followers of Jesus who were present at that last supper. However, the Biblical story does not mention or picture them.

From the time we are born, we are brainwashed into believing what is in the Bible is the truth and the light. Oh, how well I remember our ministers telling

*What God Really Wants*

us that during their sermons when I was a youngster. Now I find myself shuddering when the TV ministers of today tell us what God meant when they interpret passages in the Bible. They recite a passage and then proceed to tell us their interpretation of what God wants us to do.

I find it amazing how some ministers have the ability to interpret the Bible so well, when even other religious people have told me that Biblical scholars differ on its interpretation. I believe ministers are just like us—human—and therefore, just as capable of being wrong in the way they interpret what they read.

# Chapter 3 – Black People & Religion

***I find this especially enlightening when it comes to the way Black people praise God based on the Bible and Christianity.*** It is amazing how a race of people, brought to the United States as slaves, can believe a book taught to them by the same race of "Good Christian" people who enslaved them.

Their proud African ancestors, before being forced to leave their homeland and transported to America, never knew anything about the Jesus or Jehovah religion that the "Good Christians" practiced (a religion they subscribed to while simultaneously slaughtering and enslaving a whole race of people).

I constantly hear about how the Jewish holocaust was the greatest human tragedy in history. I say, what happened to the Black race during slavery definitely has the potential to be worst. Nobody knows exactly how many Africans died while en route to America or after arriving here.

In fact, nobody knows how many Africans died during the carnage visited upon Africans by these "Good Christians" while they were still in Africa. I am sure that many resisted and died in the process.

*What God Really Wants*

The records cannot reflect the horror these people went through at the hands of some "Good Christians." Isn't it conceivable that these people who enslaved Africans purposely taught them a religion so that they would toe the line, not rebel, and expect to be rewarded in the "Afterlife?"

Thomas Jefferson once said something about how a people without hope, is a dangerous people who eventually will rebel. The "Good Christians" knew the slaves needed something to hope for, so they gave it to them via the Bible. In my opinion, this is all you get out of religion as practiced by many religious leaders today: hope, not salvation. Blacks lived their lives in slavery, hoping to die and go to Heaven, with the belief they would finally have their paradise when they met God there.

They settled for abuse, rape, and dehumanization by a race of people who used God and their religion to justify their crimes. If I remember correctly, many White ministers were involved with their local Ku Klux Klan chapters. If they were not Klan leaders, these ministers and other "Good White Christians" were prominent members of the group.

These people preached on Sunday about how they should treat their fellow man, based on God's word in the Bible, but abused and hang their slaves on the weekdays. In fact, they did not even consider their slaves to be human beings. Even today, many religious people treat their animals (especially dogs) better than they treat their fellow man, no matter what the human's ethnicity is.

When I was a child, I remember our Black ministers telling us that the Bible says the meek shall inherit the Earth. Thinking back on it now, I believe that passage, and others like it, might have done more than anything else to keep Blacks in slavery for as long as we were. It helped create a group of people who saw some kind of hope if they remained peaceful and meek.

It created a group of docile and subservient people. I suspect that those passages were probably a regular message to Black congregations during slavery. They certainly were in the churches I attended during the 1950's and 1960's.

It is ironic that the slave masters did not want their slaves to learn to read. Could there have been a purpose for that as well? Only people who could read were able to interpret the Bible. Since slaves were unable to read, who do you suppose read and interpreted the Bible for them?

# Chapter 4 – Whom to Follow

***To those who will say I do not know what I am talking about, I agree with you 100 percent.*** That is what puzzles me as I write. When I began, I had absolutely no idea what I was about to write. I found myself feeling as if someone were telling me what to do and say. All I can tell you is that what I write is coming from my heart and with love for this world. Therefore, I will continue to write as the words come to me.

I cannot and will not ever say what I write is the absolute truth. I can only say it is how I feel and what I believe. I hope what you read will help you understand why we should live by what God represents, not by the standards as outlined in the Bible.

I repeat, men and women wrote what is in the Bible. They may have had their own biases! The God I choose to follow set standards that are not hard to attain, and are much less hurtful than some of the stories related in the Bible. In my opinion, the Bible is full of questions, threats, and untruths.

Durie Burns

For instance, take the story of Adam and Eve. It was the first story I began to question as a young man. Our church leaders told us that Adam and Eve were the first two and only people God created when he created the Heavens and the Earth. I questioned that characterization because the book of Genesis talks about what Adam and Eve did when they left the Garden of Eden and where they went. It also discusses what Cain did when he left. In both situations, the children of Adam and Eve went to another land where they were eventually married.

I say to you, if Adam and Eve were the only two people God created in the beginning, then where did these spouses come from that Cain and his siblings married? Either they were Cain's siblings or their spouses were children of someone other than Adam and Eve.

Personally, I would rather think they were children of someone other than Adam and Eve. Therefore, if there were other people on Earth in another land at the same time as Adam and Eve, it appears that our ministers, based on what they told me at church, were unfamiliar with this possibility, were misinformed by what was written, or just plain lied all these years.

Based on the Bible story, as told to me, we are all descendants of Adam and Eve. It does not matter if you are black, white, red, or yellow; you are my cousin. If you believe the story of Adam and Eve, I

*What God Really Wants*

ask you, "Why would people ever treat their relatives the way they do?" Based on the Adam and Eve story, we can only conclude that the slave masters in America enslaved their own relatives. If you believe in Genesis, then you should believe that the people in the Middle East are direct descendents of Adam and Eve.

Christians talk about their love for God, and how important he is in their lives, yet they constantly do things that are totally the opposite of what God wants us to do. They speak derogatorily about their friends, neighbors, and others. They criticize other religions because they believe in God differently. They preach forgiveness, but are quick to hold it against someone who makes a mistake. Employers will not hire people who have spent time incarcerated, when all that most of these people want is a job and an opportunity to make up for the mistake they made.

Over the years, I have discussed my interpretation of this questionable passage with numerous religious leaders and followers. Some have said, they could not explain it and others have attempted to explain it another way. Some told me that in the beginning God had indeed created other people, not just Adam and Eve. They said this information was not included in the Bible.

They told me the Catholic Church made the decision to leave that information out of the Bible.

Durie Burns

The Catholic Church assembled the Bible based on the written scrolls it possessed. Of course, this revelation just made me ask more questions.

If the Catholic Church chose to leave information out of the Bible about other people God created besides Adam and Eve, why did the church leave it out? This seems to be an important aspect overlooked by religious leaders. What else did they decide to leave out? Who authorized the Catholic Church to assemble the Bible anyway, and why?

My understanding is that King James ordered the creation of the King James Version of the Bible used by many Christians. What was King James' purpose? Therein lies the mystery for me. Maybe his purpose was to use the book to control his subjects better, maybe not.

I saw a story on the History Channel that indicated King James had his priests assemble the Bible because he needed a way to control his people. I just want you to question it for yourselves. Reasonably consider the possibility.

I really want you to understand that I, in no way, want to destroy or defame any religion. That is not my purpose. On the contrary, I hope to unite religions and their leaders and followers to do what I believe God really wants.

*What God Really Wants*

For far too long, the various religions I have come to know have fought for the right to be the one to send our souls to God. In the process, they have alienated each other and the people they serve. I could be a millionaire if I had been given a dollar every time someone told me I could not get to Heaven unless I believed in his or her particular religion.

Over the years, religious leaders of various denominations and their followers have told me I must believe in their religion in order to be saved by God and get to Heaven. But it seemed that no matter which religion I chose, I would not get to Heaven anyway because people of the other faiths would tell me I was following the wrong religion. Apparently, the only sure way I could get to Heaven was to believe in *everyone's* religion at the same time.

It got to the point that I gave up trying to follow any specific religion. Since I was not sure which religion to believe in, I became so confused that I began to question the need to believe in *any* of them. As the years passed, I decided I could believe in God, but not religion or its leaders. I decided to follow the God of respect, hope, trust, forgiveness, kindness, peace, and love for humanity; not the God of fear, mayhem, and richness as sometimes implied in the Bible and through some ministers.

Durie Burns

I have come to believe that many religious leaders today preach the word of God for their own selfish reasons and teach only those parts of the Bible that meet their needs. As one person whom I believe is a true Man of God said in one of his sermons I attended; ministers tend to preach passages from the Bible that are subject to different interpretations.

He said there are passages in the Bible that God said are "must" things for us to do. Yet, he said, preachers shy away from talking about those "must" things. He proceeded to discuss some of the "must" things in the Bible. I say to you the reason many ministers talk about the controversial things in the Bible is because they can make them sound anyway they want. However, they can only interpret the "must" things one way.

# Chapter 5 – The Jesus Business

***In South Florida, I met this true Man of God mentioned above.*** He listened to several of my thoughts and, surprisingly, agreed with a few. He and I entered into a discussion regarding ministers making money preaching the word of God. I said several of these ministers are making a mockery of God's word and desires for his people, that God is against his messengers enriching themselves at the expense of their flocks.

I told him about a minister in Buffalo, New York, who'd told me he had a minister friend who contacted a particular rich minister to see if this person would speak to his congregation. The rich minister said he would need $30,000 to even consider coming to talk to the congregation.

If he decided to come, the rich minister wanted substantially more money. Of course, this was not possible because the Buffalo minister's friend had a small congregation. The Buffalo minister also has a small congregation. I have known him since he became the minister at my parents' church after I returned to Buffalo from the military in the 1970.

Durie Burns

This Buffalo minister, in my opinion, is another minister who represents what a true Man of God should be. After 22 years, he retired from his full-time job working with the Boy Scouts of America but continued preaching, despite being ill.

In fact, I remember my mother telling me a story about this minister. She said, when he became the church leader, the elders asked him about his salary. He told them he would take $20 a month. My mother said they voted to give him $50.

Think about this: he maintained his church for over four decades, preaching God's word, according to the Bible, because that is what he believes; yet worked a full time job to support his family. He refused to live off his congregation. This Man of God, as I see him, said that this rich minister, in his opinion, was a charlatan. He further stated that the IRS should be investigating some of these ministers.

I found this very ironic since I spent my entire career working as a Special Agent for the IRS. His words rang out so clearly that I question how these people can live lavish lifestyles off the funds provided to them by their congregations and not be subject to IRS scrutiny.

I understand the tax laws make most churches exempt from taxes, but are the ministers also exempt when they profit from the money the church earns? I do not think so. Churches should set up a

*What God Really Wants*

system that pays their ministers a reasonable salary (not a fee based on the number of members the minister can generate) and let them buy their own cars, homes, etc. Why should Men of God, his messengers, live any better than the people they serve? After all, Jesus never did.

After hearing about what the Buffalo minister said, the minister from South Florida asked me if I was saying that God did not want religious leaders to make money in his name. I told him I believe that God has no objection to religious leaders acquiring money preaching his word, etc. It is how the money is used once received. I believe God is concerned about how the money is used. God wants money obtained in his name used for the people our religious leaders serve and not for the leaders themselves.

I do not want to belabor the point, but it should be one of the most important issues of today. People need to question their leaders when they see them prospering from church funds or funds generated using God's name while other people in their congregation are on welfare and living in slum conditions. Even profits earned from writing books such as this one in God's name, should go to God's people. In my case, the money should go to aid the homeless, and others, rather than me.

Let me relate to you what a church-going Christian woman told me happened to her. She attended a church function in Detroit, Michigan, where her friend was recording a gospel-music album. She and one of her sisters paid for her family, a whole row of people, to attend the function. She said they spent about two thousand dollars for the tickets. She said there had to be at least 2,000 people at this function. She was sitting in the balcony talking to a friend when the preacher started requesting an offering.

According to her, he requested those people with $100 or more to come down front to provide their offerings to God. Then, he continued downward by requesting those with $50 or more offerings to come down. From there, he went to $25, then down to $10. After all these people had come down front, the preacher requested everyone else to hold what they had in the air until it was collected.

All of a sudden, he called out the church-going woman who had not come forward or raised her hand. Keep in mind that she was in the balcony, dressed very nicely and wearing diamonds. The minister yelled to get her attention and then began to question her about why she had not raised her hand. The woman was very surprised and questioned the minister's reason for singling her out. In fact, she said she cursed the minister for his actions.

One would think this woman had already donated enough to the church's cause just by buying the tickets to this event. When a minister singles out a person because he or she does not give to the collection plate, that minister is revealing his or her true colors and greed for money.

The Jesus business has become one of the more lucrative ways to make money in today's society. There are many ministers making millions of dollars through their ministries and Christian universities. In October 2007, a story came out about the son of Oral Roberts who was diverting money from Oral Roberts University's funds for his own personal use.

What makes this story unique to me is that people actually *thought* it was unique. As an IRS Special Agent, I investigated cases involving business people using money from their businesses for personal use. This is a violation of IRS law because those people failed to pay personal taxes on the diverted income.

I believe that these ministers and so-called people of faith have been using money earned through their association with Jesus and God for their personal use for years. I am willing to bet that if someone were to investigate all ministers who have control of mega churches and/or live lavish lifestyles, the investigator would find that the ministers' misuse of funds obtained through their association with their faith is a common practice.

Durie Burns

People should question the need for religious leaders to have expensive cars, large and oversized homes, airplanes, etc., especially, those who stockpile assets purchased through funds earned in God's name—while people in their congregation are in need. I saw a TV program about a mega-church minister who not only owned two airplanes but owned the airport as well. I found this to be a bit excessive. This minister, in my opinion, is a "False Prophet." His goal is not God's goal for him or his congregation. I understand Congress, at one point, investigated this minister.

Now, I am not suggesting that ministers shouldn't earn enough money to live on. I am talking about all money earned, after expenses, using God or your religious affiliation; whether you do so using Not-for-Profit or For-Profit ventures. You cannot separate the two. **God wants his people to share the use of money earned in his name based on your status as his messenger.**

Over the years, I have asked several ministers about rich ministers who do things only for money, and they all tell me that they are aware of these ministers. When I ask why they do not do anything about them, I never get a clear answer. Usually, I get an answer like this: "Well, he'll be dealt with when he goes to meet his maker." I find this answer to be so repulsive. After all, these ministers are living the "Good Life" while the people they serve are suffering.

*What God Really Wants*

I am telling you what I have told all those ministers I have met who say they are true believers of God; "God wants his true Men and Women of God to stop those ministers who take money from their followers and use it to enrich themselves." Once you choose to minister in the name of God, you must walk in the path of righteousness. There is no if, and, or but here. Otherwise, you are no different from the false prophets talked about in the Bible.

Do not walk in the life if you cannot live the life. I grant you that religious leaders are human; however, they cannot act like other humans. That is the sacrifice they must make if they are to preach in the name of God. They must respect the path they have chosen and honor it by being oblivious to the human temptations of the world. That includes enriching themselves.

The following story may be out of place, but I had to include it somewhere. It has to do with the Buffalo minister who I said previously is a true Man of God. I contacted him in April 2007. I told him I was coming to Buffalo and wanted first to verify, over the telephone, the story about a certain rich minister he had told me about at my father's funeral in Buffalo in 2004.

That story, written previously, is what he verified that day. I told him about this book and shared a few of the stories in it. I told him I was not going to mention his name or anyone else's name in the

## Durie Burns

book. I said I was going to contact him when I arrived in Buffalo the following Thursday so we could visit on Friday. I wanted to share what I had already written in order to get his opinion.

I arrived in Buffalo approximately eight days later, on a Thursday, and found out that the Buffalo minister had passed away unexpectedly before I arrived. I was in shock when I found out because I did not know about his death until I read a notice in Thursday's paper while I was eating breakfast on Friday morning. I was going to call the minister as soon as I finished breakfast and reading the paper.

The last section of the paper I came to was the obituary. I do not usually read obituaries, but for some reason, I felt compelled to read it. I remember thinking I should read it since I have not been in Buffalo for a while. I did it because something inside me told me I might see someone I knew in it. Never in my wildest dream did I think it would be the Buffalo minister.

The article said they were viewing his body that day. I quickly got dressed and went to the church to see him. It was as if I were walking in a dream. I could not believe this man had left Earth with still so much he wanted to do. His best friend in the church—a man whom the minister had told about my visit to discuss the book—revealed some startling things to me about the minister.

*What God Really Wants*

He told me that Reverend Whitfield Washington, Jr., had always put others ahead of himself during his church life, participating in numerous activities with other organizations and with the children in the congregation. His friend asked me if I knew how much the church paid the minister. He said, "We paid this man $50 a week." That is how he said it. Reverend Washington had been the pastor of his church for 35 years, since 1972.

Think about that in today's time of preaching and millionaire ministries. Now maybe you can see why I consider Reverend Washington a true Man of God. This is what God asked of his ministers. Sacrifice for the welfare of others, not others sacrificing for your welfare.

I learned more revelations about Reverend Whitfield Washington, Jr., at his funeral. As always at funerals, people praise the deceased, and we often do not know if everything they say is what they say it is. However, when one of Reverend Washington's children went to the podium to address the congregation, I was shocked again. I turned to my friend sitting next to me. I said, "I didn't know the Reverend had a White wife." My friend said he did not but that Reverend Washington had adopted a White child and raised him.

This man raised by Reverend Washington said that people always say you should not marry a woman with a ready-made family. He continued by saying that Reverend Washington had not only married a woman with three children; they had one of their own and had adopted him off the street.

He further stated that we should not let anyone tell us that Blacks and Whites cannot cohabitate because his family had done it. When I asked my friend what the adopted son did for a living, he said he was a doctor. That is when I decided to include this story and tell you who this true Man of God from Buffalo was.

Reverend Whitfield Washington, Jr., deserves recognition for his dedication to his family, his church, the Boy Scouts of America, and for all the lives he touched throughout his short life. You see, Reverend Washington, Jr., was sixty-four years old when he passed away. His passing will not be in vain if I can help it.

I will do all I can to honor this man for as long as I live. My only regret is that I had not followed this man and walked with him. If I had, I might have truly known his greatness. At least I have a reference point from which to work regarding what to expect of our religious leaders. Reverend Washington left me with that, and it might be his greatest gift to me.

As I stated earlier, I have had numerous discussions with people of faith, including ministers. Usually, these discussions included my telling them about

*What God Really Wants*

my concern regarding ministers and religious leaders who earn enormous amounts of money and use it for their personal gain. Most, if not all, have agreed with me that it is wrong to do what some leaders are doing.

I discussed the issue with a person of faith who used to preach the word of God. He said he no longer was preaching but he is still much involved in the church. Our discussion led us to the topic of ministers who seemed to have profited from spreading what they called God's word.

He told me he felt Jesus could have been more financially rich than these ministers could, because he was more powerful than they are and had more followers. But, he said, Jesus never opted to make himself financially rich off the word of God. In fact, he chose to do just the opposite.

When I asked him what he would do, he said something that made good sense to me. He said he would do what Jesus did. He said, "As a person of faith when tempted, I would think, "What would Jesus do?" I believe God is telling me to tell you he wants us to think, "What would Jesus do," when our decision times come.

# Chapter 6 – The Catholic Church and Wealth

***Think about it.*** The Catholic Church is like a big business with its own CEO (the Pope). People have told me the Pope runs the Vatican like a government. That he lives in a palace with goblets of gold and silver. (I have never personally seen the Vatican; and probably never will). If this is true, then what makes the Pope any different from the rest of the rich and greedy men in our world today? According to some of his followers, the Pope has extensive assets at his disposal. Sounds like a corporation to me.

Will someone please explain to me what gives the Catholic Church the right to establish the Pope as the world leader for religion? I have yet to read or hear anything in the Bible about the Pope. The people who wrote the Bible, which God supposedly influenced, did not write anything about a Pope.

In my opinion, the Pope and his influence over world religion was not in God's plan when the scrolls used by the Catholic Church were included

*What God Really Wants*

in the Bible. If I am right, then why do people hold this person/position in such high esteem?

When allegations were made that numerous priests had molested male children, impregnated nuns, and generally run amuck in their parishes, where was the Pope? Until the spring or summer of 2010, I do not recall ever hearing any Pope express his displeasure with the cover-ups his priests conducted to prevent discovery of these incidents. In fact, he did not even kick them out of the church.

The Church simply moved these priests from one parish to another. The Pope didn't do anything about it. His inaction made it easier for the priests to get away with their crimes. He helped facilitate the additional cover-up crimes by not taking the appropriate action other citizens are required to take under similar circumstances by our law enforcement agencies. Ordinary people would be prosecuted if they had information about crimes being committed and failed to report them.

I believe strong consideration should be given to the idea of prosecuting the Pope, Cardinals, and any other church followers who were aware of these atrocities towards children and others. I once read an article which said a priest had actually told the current Pope, when the Pope was a Cardinal, about a priest who had molested someone. The future Pope did nothing but move the child-molesting priest to another diocese.

Durie Burns

It is apparent that our law-enforcement agencies turned a blind-eye to this matter because of their religious beliefs. They refused to investigate the Pope and Cardinals for their massive cover-ups, which have been going on in the Catholic Church for decades. They should arrest them all for helping criminals evade the law. These church fathers, being fully knowledgeable about what was going on, allowed perverts the opportunity to be around other children. The Catholic Church became a place for perverts to hide and commit criminal acts and avoid prosecution from the law.

It is the biggest conspiracy I have ever seen. I cannot believe the same thing would happen to any child molester's family if that family concealed the pervert's activities from the world. If the molester were caught, the family members who had knowledge of the conspiracy would be arrested and jail, too.

This type of crime occurred in the state of Georgia a few years ago. Someone in a family of three kidnapped, raped, and killed a little boy. The police arrested the father, mother, and son for the crime. All three were charged, because either they actually did the crime or tried to cover up the crime.

What makes these incidents involving Catholic leaders any different? Why do we allow them to traumatize our young and still be able to preach the word of God? What makes the people of the world

*What God Really Wants*

tolerate the abuses of religious leaders, especially those in the Catholic Church, but not stand for the same behavior by the general public?

And what did the Pope do when the pressure to rectify these wrongs became too great? He authorized settlement agreements. I know of at least one such agreement in Boston for $50 million. In July 2007, the Catholic Church agreed to a $680 million settlement in Los Angeles, California. In addition, a month or so later, they agreed to a $200 million settlement in the San Diego area. I understand there is documented evidence that the Catholic Church has been settling sexual-assault lawsuits since at least 1952.

I once asked a Catholic friend how the Pope could come up with $50 million just like that. He said from the church's assets, which they probably liquidated. To my surprise, he further stated that this amount was just a drop in the bucket for the Pope. I realized the truth of that statement when I saw the Catholic Church had $930 million in 2007 to settle just three lawsuits. **Let's see; cover up a crime by paying money to the victims—what a way for "Good Christians" to act.** How many more have they settled and/or will they settle before people see them for what they really are?

I do not know about you, but I refuse to believe that God would want his messenger to set himself up as a King. As far as I am concerned, the Pope is exactly what Moses was upset about when he went to the mountain and returned with the 10 Commandments. The Catholic Church worships the Pope as if he were a God. They allow him to live as if he were a King.

I refuse to believe that God would want his messengers to enrich their lives this way. I understand that the Pope and the Catholic Church gives money to various charities and help some people. The issue I have is this: why are the Pope and the Catholic Church holding assets worth billions of dollars when there are so many people in need in every country throughout the world?

The Pope should use the money and assets, hoarded by the Catholic Church, for the good of the world's people who are in need. Isn't that what you would expect from Jesus, if he had had this kind of money in his day? After all, the Church generated the money through donations and other religious functions. Even if they invested the money and it earned interest, the entire amount should be considered funds earned in God's name and donated back to the people in need, not be held, for whatever reason, as assets.

They talk about the Pope as if he is the most important religious leader in the free world. He gives out advice and rules the Catholic Church as if he were a King. I understand that the Vatican even

*What God Really Wants*

has its own army. I need someone to explain to me why the Pope needs an army.

Why would a man of God need to defend himself against anyone or anything? Jesus had no army and never did anything to defend himself against those who sought to destroy him. I believe the Pope needs his army to protect the extensive valuables the Catholic Church has obtained and hoarded over the years.

Just before the start of the 2008 national presidential election, I even heard a man—a religious Republican—say on Fox news that the Pope is like God on Earth. This statement is as far from the truth as it can be.

I still cannot understand the rationale for the Pope's existence in religion. Maybe I am wrong, but, again, I have not found anything in the Bible about establishing the Papal position in religion. I even asked my minister friend from South Florida where it says there should be a Pope in the Bible. He told me he had never heard of it.

Yet, the Catholic Church determined which scrolls to use to create the passages to formulate the Bible. People told me that there were many other scrolls in their possession, but they were not included in the Bible. I have always wondered what is contained in those scrolls and why they were not worthy enough to be included. Maybe, because they contain messages that do not agree with what the Catholic Church wanted us to hear? Man manipulates man in many ways.

I heard that several Black ministers of mega churches are hiring bodyguards. When I heard it, I was not surprised since they probably need protection to ensure that no one takes their windfall profits. But, if they hired these bodyguards for physical protection, then I have a problem with that, too. The problem I have is that ministers are always saying God will provide for all our needs; that we should put our faith in God.

No minister should be afraid of or be concerned about physical violence because they should be placing their faith in God and, therefore, have no fear of any man. If they hire bodyguards, then they are showing us that they do not have enough faith that God will protect them. This is another example of "Do as I say, not as I do."

# Chapter 7 – Religious Leaders and Crime

*I believe religious leaders get away with committing criminal acts and adultery because people hold them up high on a pedestal.* People tend to idolize these leaders. The more power that some ministers gain over their church and followers, the more opportunities they have to abuse that power.

When caught, these leaders expect forgiveness from their followers. After all, haven't they preached this sermon repeatedly throughout the years? Shouldn't you forgive them because they are "only human?" I cannot tell you how many times people have told me that these criminal ministers are "only human." It is such a feeble excuse for bad behavior, like shrugging off the behavior of bad children by claiming, "Boys will be boys."

Granted, religious leaders are no more saintly than you or I. However, just as there is no excuse for you or me to commit any serious violations of the law, criminal or moral, so too is there no excuse for a minister or representative of God to forsake his or her own preaching and commit any serious violation of law, criminal or moral.

In the spring of 2005, I read a newspaper article about a Jacksonville, Florida, minister convicted of having a two-year ongoing sexual relationship with a young girl, a member of his church, who was eleven when the affair began.

Several things bothered me as I read the story. First, the church followers, including the girl's mother and other relatives, were in court pleading on behalf of the minister at his sentencing. I was very shocked by this conduct. How could the child's mother support a man who had raped her daughter?

And it *was* rape, make no mistake, for, even if the sex had been "consensual"—and that's doubtful when it's a matter of someone in a position of authority and power coercing a younger, more powerless individual—an eleven year old is well below the age of consent. The mother and the congregation asked the judge to be lenient and not to sentence the minister to jail. How could the congregation support such a villain? This was just the first detail that shocked me.

Next, at least one member of the congregation asked the judge to consider leniency because when the minister took over as pastor of their church, they had only about 60 members; now, they had over 350 members.

*What God Really Wants*

The mother and the congregants even told the judge they wanted the minister to return as pastor of their church once he served his sentence. How outrageous is that? I thought the judge should have convicted them all for conspiracy. They had to have known about the affair long before the arrest of the minister.

Well, you will not guess what the judge did and said. He sentenced the minister to 18 months in jail and then told the congregation that when the minister returned to pastor their church, it would be up to the congregation to keep him away from the children. What kind of asinine thing is that?

We all need to have a quick head check if we truly believe such a thing is acceptable. If you think God wants his messengers to commit acts of this nature, that God endorses such behavior, and that these messengers should still be able to preach his word after committing such acts, you are ridiculous.

Every member of that church should be ashamed for supporting this minister. The judge should have sentenced this man to jail for many more years and never allow him to be around children again.

I believe there are laws that prevent child molesters from being within a certain number of feet from a school where children attend. If so, then how could a judge even begin to do and say what this judge did? The judge should never allow this man to preach again, especially if he is going to be around children. The man is a criminal and a child molester. They should show his identity on the websites that identifies these people so everyone will know.

This minister, in my opinion, received undue leniency from the judge and the congregation. God does not want us to forgive ministers for their crimes any more than we would any other human being. God's messengers are supposed to be reliable, honorable and above all else, trustworthy.

Committing deceitful and despicable moral or criminal acts while allegedly preaching God's word makes you worse than any person I can fathom. Such people are lower than serial rapists and murderers. They prey on our children's trust and respect in order to indulge in their perverted sexual needs. They are to be treated no different from any other person who commits such acts. These leaders, while setting themselves up to be trusted, violate that trust and then ask for forgiveness. What a crock of bull!

I have seen repeated instances where religious leaders got into trouble and people of faith made excuses for them and continued to support them. There have been so many of these incidents in the past few years that I do not know where to start listing them. I know that the first time I encountered

*What God Really Wants*

this behavior was when I was a teenager going to church in Buffalo, New York.

I remember an usher who always seemed to keep his eye on me during church service, ever since I was a child. It seemed to me he singled me out when we misbehaved. I was afraid of this man because he seemed so holy. Because he always tried to make me pay attention to the minister, I guess I thought he was someone special in the church.

Then, one day, I heard they had arrested this usher in a bank robbery. What a shock! I could not believe that this man, a representative of God, had done something so criminal. This may have been my first revelation that so-called "Good Christians/Men of God" could, do the same things as other men. The difference is that "Good Christians/Men of God" expect, or in some cases demand, instant forgiveness from their peers and followers.

However, I believe that Men of God must hold themselves up to a higher standard than other men. (When I say "Men of God," I also mean *Women* of God). But writing "Men and Women of God" every time is too time consuming, so I'm using the one to stand for both.

Men of God should not do what other men do. How can they tell us what not to do if they're going to commit the same transgressions themselves? How could I believe their preaching then? How could I forgive them? Would you forgive me if it were your son or daughter I molested?

Again, I say, people who hold themselves out to be messengers of God cannot allow themselves the luxury of "just being human." They must live a more humble life as did Jesus. I know I might be redundant saying this, but I cannot impress enough upon our leaders the need for them to understand this fact.

Religious leaders set themselves up to be holy and spiritual. To me, this means they should be what we aspire to emulate. They represent all that is sacred and right to the children of the world. As children and adults, we are influenced by what they say and do. If our religious leaders are continually committing crimes themselves, how can they honestly preach the word of God and have us believe them?

Religious Leaders must reject the desire to be rich. Men of God should offer up a substantial amount of their assets—whether that money is earned through preaching or by some other means—to their church or for religious activities or other good and Godlike works. Likewise, their followers must attempt to share their riches. I say, "attempt" because you cannot hold all people to the same standard as religious leaders.

*What God Really Wants*

However, if you profess yourself to be a Bible-toting religious person, the same standards required of our religious leaders should apply to you. In all of society, it should play out that way. All of us—who have means—must share with our fellow human beings until no one in this world is hungry or lacks the necessities of life to live.

Religious leaders must work to provide shelter for everyone, and everyone should have the right to medical care. Religious leaders must not engage in activities that are unlawful, especially when it comes to the treatment of our children. I believe this is what God really wants. What these Catholic priests and other religious leaders have done has destroyed the lives of young children. **To me, there is no greater crime, including murder, than a crime against a child.**

# Chapter 8 – War and Religion

***We have wasted so much money on wars and diplomatic summits—all of which only accomplishes one thing: wasting money.*** We never accomplish anything, nothing changes. We seem to go from one war to another, from one nation to another, just slaughtering people in the name of God. **Let me say this loud and clear: I do not care what you say—*GOD DOES NOT CONDONE WAR!***

In case you have not heard, war kills. I believe that no true religion of God (be he called Jehovah, Allah, Jesus, etc.) can ever practice hatred and killing. The God I choose to follow is a compassionate God who wants people of this world to share in the beauty he provided.

If you believe that God created this Earth and all that is in it, then you need to believe he meant for us all to share in it as equally as possible. I know this is shocking to people of influence and financial wealth. I know this will cause many of you to disagree with what I write. However, I expect you to disagree.

*What God Really Wants*

You think it is fine to preach or listen to the gospel, go to church on Sunday, Monday, Tuesday, Wednesday, Thursday, Friday, or Saturday (pick any or all of them) and then go home to all your riches while people are suffering and dying all over the world. How hypocritical is that?

I say to such people, you are not true followers of God. You have become what God told Moses to stop. In biblical times, people had become corrupt, jaded, and crooked; they worshiped idol Gods, and so forth. Sound familiar? I see the same thing happening now as back then, yet nobody is trying to stop it.

If President Bush really believed in God, and what God wants, he would never have considered attacking another country. Yes, in this world, we have to defend ourselves if attacked, but we do not have to kill innocent people because someone made us mad. I do not condone what Al-Qaeda did and believe we had a right to be upset. Their God does not want them to attack us either. We have to consider options other than war.

Iraq did not attack the United States. Osama Ben Laden and Al-Qaeda attacked us. All we heard from the government concerning the war was how many Al-Qaeda fighters and insurgents we have killed in Iraq. They said it with a lot of pride. From the beginning, they even had a hit list of those whom they wanted hunted down and killed.

Durie Burns

We could avoid all this retaliation if all nations were to practice what I believe is the true word of God. There would be nothing to retaliate for, if we truly practiced God's word. There would not have been a 9/11 attack if the world truly believed as God wants us to do.

Each side in President Bush's war said it was fighting because of their belief in their God, as if it were what their God wanted them to do. They actually talked as if God wanted them to kill or die in his name.

These people are definitely going about it the wrong way. God wants us to sit down and talk rationally about how we can help each other survive better. God wants us to love our fellow man—no matter what his color, nationally, religious belief, or sexual orientation.

Iraqi insurgents, to me, were no different from the American patriots who stood up for their country and its way of life during our War of Independence from Britain. If Russia had attacked America during the Cold War, what would we have done? Every loyal American who believed in our way of life would have resisted to the end. During those times, Russia also believed their way of life was the best for our world.

Well, what do you think the Iraqi people were doing? They were defending their way of life. We

*What God Really Wants*

have no more right to force democracy on them than Hitler did when he tried to force his beliefs and his way of life on the German people and ultimately on the rest of the world.

How can anyone claim to be one with God and be proud of murdering people? In this war, America has substantially killed or caused to be killed more civilians than were killed by the attack on the World Trade Center by Al-Qaeda on September 11, 2001. Yet, President Bush continued to pursue this war so aggressively that he could not see that he was invoking God's name in vain.

At one point, I heard a Republican say that Bush believed we were fighting the devil in Iraq. He claimed to be fighting Al-Qaeda in Iraq. Prior to the attack on Iraq, we were in hot pursuit of Al-Qaeda in Afghanistan and Pakistan.

There was no evidence of Al-Qaeda in Iraq prior to our invasion of that country. In fact, Saddam Hussein would not allow terrorists in Iraq. We attacked Iraq because we claimed that country had weapons of mass destruction. Once it was determine the weapons did not exist, the justification for the attack changed drastically.

Bush decided to stay the course in order to bring democracy to Iraq. He said we were now in Iraq to liberate the people. There was no mention of liberating the Iraqi people until we could not find any weapons of mass destruction; and could no longer justify the mistake we made by invading Iraq in the first place.

The devil is not in Iraq and never was. If the devil is any place, it is in the hearts and minds of men such as Osama Bin Laden and George W. Bush. These two people have been the main perpetrators of some of the most intimidating military events in my lifetime.

Osama Bin Laden attacked us without just cause or provocation. George W. Bush did the same thing to Iraq. Each believed the other was trying to destroy his country's way of life. It is funny because Bin Laden believes he was fighting the devil in the United States.

How can followers of God believe they are both fighting the devil by fighting each other? If this were the case, at least one, if not both, would have to be wrong. God wants you to know they are both wrong.

We as a people worldwide must stand up and stop this madness before it is too late. The world must demand an end to this need to occupy other lands. We must help each other. If we do not, our future might be in great jeopardy.

We should never make *war* and God synonymous. However, the Bible did so. So many books in the

*What God Really Wants*

Bible talk about war and about God supporting those wars. It sounds to me that some people who promoted war may have written some of these passages to justify their slaughter of so many people—many of them innocent of any wrongdoing but caught up in the fight. It is ironic how history is seemingly repeating itself.

# Chapter 9 – God and Gay People

***I know this will be a very controversial topic and religious leaders are going to point out there is at least one passage in the Bible that indicates God is against homosexuality.*** Many religious leaders informed me of this "fact." However, I strongly disagree with this part of the Bible. I am not gay nor do I condone being gay. I just do not think my God cares about your sexual orientation.

Remember, my premise for this book is that the Bible has many untruths in it. This notion that God would hold something against someone just because of his or her sexual preference is extremely ridiculous. Who we sleep with does not matter. It is what we do when we are not home alone that counts. God asks very little of us.

He wants us to believe there is only one God (which most religious people do). He wants us to share the wealth and end the hunger and homelessness in the world. He wants us to provide for the needy until there are no more people in need. He wants us to serve humanity as if it were the only way to get into Heaven.

*What God Really Wants*

I believe God loves gay people just as much as he loves other people. I refuse to believe otherwise. Since I believe God loves all people, I have to believe he loves gay people just as much as he loves me. I do not know how many years have gone by since the beginning of the world, but I will bet there have been gay people around since the beginning of time.

We may not want to think about it, but we need to question the reasons given for God's supposed dislike of gay people. How can people of God hate others, gay or otherwise? Why do religious people and their leaders talk about love for your fellow man and then discriminate against people because they are different from them?

It is because they are paranoid. Their ancestors trained them to believe this fallacy, all because someone, whom we have never met, wrote in a particular book (the Bible) that homosexuality was wrong. Could it have been his own personal belief and not God's word when he wrote it?

It just does not make sense to me that some religious leaders have actually refused to allow gay people to join their church. God wants us to embrace all people no matter what their difference. God wants us to embrace each other as his creations.

Durie Burns

If God has a plan for us here on Earth, as some Christians tell me they believe, then what was his plan for gay people? Do you think he put them here to piss you off? No, if you believe God has a plan for us, then you have to believe he had no problem with gay people. God wants you to know that gay people are no different from the rest of us.

So-called "God-fearing" people have told me so many different things about God and what God wants that I have become very confused. One religion will tell me one thing and another tells me differently to fit the teaching philosophy of their particular religion.

At least one religion preaches that, in order to get into Heaven, you must repent all your sins, have faith in God, and live by "good Christian values." Another religion says you must believe in the Jehovah and live Jehovah's way to have any chance of getting into Heaven. If I am not a believer in Jehovah, but am a Christian, does this mean I cannot get into Heaven? I do not think so.

If so, what happened to all those people who lived before your particular religion existed? What happened to the Indians in North America or the Africans in Africa who did not even know the Bible? For centuries, the American Indians believed in several gods (e.g., the Sun God, Moon God, etc.).

*What God Really Wants*

Now, it is common belief that these Indian gods do not exist. However, this was the religion taught to them by their ancestors. Were the Indians right or wrong to believe in these gods? Per my Christians, it would mean no Indians who believed in their gods are in Heaven. They would have had no chance of getting there because their ancestors told them untruths.

My question: have we, as Christians, Catholics, Jehovah Witnesses, etc. been lied to by our ancestors and those who preached the ancient words in the Bible? Our ancestors told us to believe in the Bible, but my experience says so many religions believe in it differently. I do not understand why. How can it mean so many different things to so many people?

Now, getting back to the biblical story that God is against homosexuality. Is this what God said, or could it be the personal desire of the person who allegedly wrote that particular scroll? Since this scroll met the need of the people who decided what went into the Bible, it was included. However, I do not believe that God would not allow anyone into his domain based on his or her sexual preference. If so, this is not the God I want to follow.

I do not believe Jesus would have turned his back on anyone because of his or her sexual preference. I believe God only cares that we believe in him and no other God. Why would God care if you were straight or gay? The fact is, "he *doesn't!*"

The people who care about making homosexuality a religious issue are those who are homophobic and very insecure. God loves all people, not just the rich and famous or the elite of the world. Jesus would be cringing over this whole issue of homosexuality if he were alive on Earth today.

I believe Jesus would welcome homosexuals into his band of disciples just as easily as he would you or me. I refuse to believe Jesus would discriminate against any living human being or other animal. We as a nation and world need to get over it and welcome all people into our churches, synagogues, military, etc.

It amazes me that Americans are fighting over the gay-rights issue. So many of those who fight gay rights are the same religious people who preach we are all God's children. I guess we are all his children unless we do something our religious leaders disagree with.

Our government leaders are battling over this issue of gays in the military. They finally acquiesced, and have allowed gays to serve openly. I say that gays have just as much right to defend and die for their country as anyone else. They have the same abilities and are just as smart as the rest of us. So, what is the big deal about them being in the military?

*What God Really Wants*

I will tell you what the big deal is—it's with the people who serve with the gay soldiers. Those "Good Christians" who think they know what is right and wrong. Maybe they and our military leaders are afraid that homosexuals in the armed services will turn our entire army gay. I served in the military and do not see that serving with homosexuals is a problem. I and thousands of heterosexuals like me went into the military and came away –straight- unaffected by the "disease" of gayness.

Even if the homosexuals were somehow able to make the rest of us as gay as they are, it wouldn't make any difference. These "transformed" soldiers would still be able to fight and die for you war mongrels, just like anyone else. If gay people want to sacrifice their lives for unjust wars, then I say let them do it. This is also their country.

God loves all people, and I truly believe God will love you and allow you to sit with him in Heaven whether you are straight or gay. I say to the gay people of the world, continue to believe in God. He has not forsaken you, and he never will—unlike the religious leaders who lie to their congregation by vilifying homosexuals.

In time, God will reveal himself to us again. That is what I recall they told me as a child. When he does, I hope that we as a people will have recognized that God will judge us by our deeds, by the kindness we

Durie Burns

have shown to all, and not by whom we sleep with or how much money we have.

# Chapter 10 – Stop the Madness

***To those who might say that I am crazy, I say to them that I am crazy.*** I am crazy to be writing this book when I know there might be people who would want to harm me because I said something that offended them. I want to assure you that I am not writing this book to offend any person, place or thing. I believe that something is influencing me to do the same thing as those who wrote the Bible passages. Someone has to do something to try to stop the madness that is going on in this world by leaders who use God's name in vain.

To those who might say I am the devil, I say to them that what I have witnessed over the years in the name of God is incredible. Men and women of faith have attributed murder, war, disabilities, storms, greed, and many other horrors to God. I find it hard to believe that God would do these things, particularly when I consider the so-called reasons given by the people who claim that God was responsible for these atrocities.

No one has ever told me that Jesus harmed a soul while he was on Earth. However, I have heard that Jesus preached and healed the sick. Jesus, to me, was a kind man who went out of his way to help those in need. In addition, no one has ever told me that Jesus made himself financially rich by preaching the word of God. Yet many religious leaders of all faiths have made themselves financially rich preaching God's word.

Sometimes, I wonder if there is a devil. One thing I do know is that I am neither the devil nor God. I am just a man saying what he believes, whether you like it or not, whether it causes me harm or not. We as a people must decide what is important. Is it important to stop the turmoil in the world over land, oil, freedom, etc. when people are dying? Is it important to refuse to talk to people who differ from us? **Is it important for the world to survive? Because I believe this is "what God *really wants*."**

If you believe it is important to stop the turmoil in the world, to talk to others who are different, and to ensure the world's survival, we must take steps to end all wars now. We must provide land, food, shelter, etc. to all people. I make this request to all religious leaders and followers so that we may someday stop the madness and make the world the way God wanted it to be when he created it.

# Chapter 11 – God's Blessings

***Here I go again, talking about money and ministers' requests to you to support their church by giving an offering to God in exchange for blessings.*** First, I want to say that God does not need your offering. God does not require you to send him money in order to receive a blessing. However, there are ministers of at least one faith (Christianity) who have made a business out of telling people they can receive a blessing from God if they send money to the ministers.

One such minister on a TV program made regular requests for your donations in exchange for a blessing from God. Currently, he has stop calling it a blessing from God. I believe he now calls it, "Planting a Seed." Why we believe these people, I have no idea.

One day, while I was watching his program, it featured a Black female who stated she heard this man's message many times and finally decided to send him a check. She stated that she and her husband had wanted to buy a home for their children and hoped that God would bless them with a home.

Durie Burns

Immediately after mailing the check at the post office, they decided to take a different route home, and, along the way, they saw a home up for sale. They eventually ended up purchasing the home and credited their purchase to the blessing from God they must have received by mailing in the money.

How ridiculous does this sound to you? It sounds extremely ridiculous to me. The minister had not even received the money yet. So how could they think he blessed them or even that God blessed them with the ability to purchase this home? In fact, the check was still in the mailbox outside the post office when she found the house. The only thing that happened is they decided to choose a different route home and ended up purchasing a home that they already had the ability to pay for *before* they sent the money.

I believe that churches need money to operate and that we, as members, should do all we can to ensure that they get these operating funds. However, there is no need to give 10% of your earnings to your church. God will bless you whether you give 10% or not. Never tie God's blessings to money. Blessings from God come from believing in him and sacrificing for others, not from how much money you give to your church, church leaders, or pastor.

Someone told me that one rich minister has two or three ATM machines outside his church. If this is true, then he is the type of minister God wants you to question. I understand this minister lives in a multi-million-dollar home, has two Rolls Royce, and an airplane. He also has a mega church with over 30,000 members. I could be wrong, but why is God so good to this minister, but not to the people he serves?

# Chapter 12 – Mega Churches

***Mega churches are the kind of churches we must look into to question their true reason for existing.*** I say this because it seems impossible for the mega-church leaders to know their constituents. I experienced this in the summer of 2006 when we buried my nephew in Charlotte, North Carolina. He was a member of a mega church, but his mother was not. She attended a much smaller church in Charlotte, where the funeral took place.

At the funeral, two ministers spoke. One was a minister from my nephew's church and the other was from his mother's church. The minister from the mother's church spoke first and admitted he did not know my nephew. I had no problem with this fact because my nephew did not attend his church. However, when the minister from my nephew's mega church got up and admitted he did not know my nephew either, I was incensed.

How could this man come to speak at my nephew's funeral and not know who he was? How can any church minister have members in whom he does do not take a personal interest—whom he doesn't bother to get to know? If a minister does not know

*What God Really Wants*

the members in his congregation, then that congregation is too big for him and/or his associate ministers. If a person donates money to your church, you should at least be able to say you met that person at least once. You should be able to relate at least one conversation you had with that person.

It was an insult to my nephew and his family for this man to represent his mega church and not know my nephew. That mega church and its leaders should be ashamed of themselves for not taking the time to know my nephew. What they showed me is that they do not care about who their members are as much as they care about the money their members generate for them.

I related this story to a person who asked me to attend her church in Jacksonville, Florida. I asked if she belonged to a mega church because she said they had over 300 members in their choir. It had to be a mega church if the choir was that big.

Defending her church, and the whole mega-church concept, she said that my nephew should have made a point to get to know his ministers at his mega church. I politely corrected the woman by saying that it should be the other way around. **"Ministers of all churches must make it a point to get to know their church members."**

Durie Burns

Ministers must remember that they are servants of the people within their church and as such, make the effort to know each of them. If you are a minister of a church and you attend a funeral for one of your members, be sure you know his or her name and something about the person. Otherwise, just stay away because you do the deceased, the family, and the friends a disservice as well as your church.

In the past, I have talked to different ministers about mega churches and their existence within the Black community. Most tell me they do not agree with mega churches and how they operate. However, again, these ministers are not willing to stand up and denounce those ministers who have created these shrines to themselves so they can obtain as much money as they can.

A cousin of mine related a story to me years ago about a minister of a mega church in Atlanta, Georgia, who, while passing the collection plate, stated he wanted to receive "quiet money." I asked my cousin what the minister meant by "quiet money?" She stated he wanted paper money, no change. At the time, I thought this was a bit much. When ministers start telling you how they want you to donate your money, you need to think about their true purpose in life.

Are they truly believers in God's word or do they have an ulterior motive for their preaching?

*What God Really Wants*

I could go on for days talking about mega churches. However, I will spare you the boredom and just say that mega churches, in my opinion, are set up for ministers to become rich. Every minister I know of with a mega church appears to have riches unlike other ministers. I believe there is a direct correlation between mega churches and rich ministers.

# Chapter 13 – Religion and Politics

*Here is another area where some ministers have done a disservice to their followers and even those who do not follow them.* Specifically, I'm speaking of those Black and other minority ministers who bought into President Bush's program that provides money to certain churches. I believe they called it the President's "Faith-Based Initiative." I must admit I do not know what it takes to receive money via this initiative. However, I do know that it has made a difference in American politics since its inception.

It made a difference in the results of the Presidential election of 2004. That year, the percentage of Black, Hispanic, and Asian votes for the Republican Presidential candidate increased significantly when compared to the 2000 election. In the 2000 election, the Republican Presidential candidate received approximately 9 percent of the Black vote, 35 percent of the Hispanic vote, and 41 percent of the Asian vote.

In the 2004 election, he received approximately 11 percent of the Black votes, 44 percent of the Hispanic vote and 43 percent of the Asian vote. The total percentage reflected an increase of approximately 13 percent in the four years since this initiative began.

I suggest the increase occurred because through this initiative, the Republicans essentially paid some Black and other minority ministers to solicit the minority vote for George W. Bush. A Bush confidant who was there when the initiative idea went into effect said as much. He stated publicly on television that the administration designed the initiative in order to obtain more of the religious vote.

It worked like a charm. Even if one can attribute the increase in only the Black and Hispanic vote to this initiative, the administration was successful. The President barely won the election even with this increased vote. Thus, if it weren't for his "Faith-Based Initiative", George W. Bush may not have been re-elected. Blacks and other minorities in America owe their current situation to our ministers who encouraged their flock to vote for Mr. Bush.

His actions during Hurricane Katrina, or should I say his *lack* of action after the hurricane, showed he did not care about what happened to Blacks and other minorities in America. His Faith-Based Initiative was successful in getting him elected, and then he deserted us. I hope those ministers who received money from him are enjoying their fruits of evil. They took a bite of the apple and sold their souls for money.

Blacks and other minorities are not the only ones who should take a hit because they allowed politics to enter their religion. Whites have been doing it for years. Certain religious leaders and followers have donated thousands of dollars of their congregations' funds to support the candidate of their choice because they believe that this or that candidate's attitude toward life, God, and morality matches their own desires and their religion's viewpoint on these subjects.

We see this every day when religious leaders try to influence the decision on whether a woman should be able to have an abortion. The religious right believes it is wrong to kill a fetus but has no problem killing that fetus once it has grown up. How hypocritical is that? If you do not believe in abortion, then you should not believe in the death penalty for the same reasons.

People who run for political office should refrain from espousing their religion or their religious beliefs during their campaigns. We elect politicians to represent all of the people in their district, city, state, or country. Therefore, their religion should be a personal thing and should not influence the decisions that affect us all.

*What God Really Wants*

Religious leaders should avoid becoming politicians because it is a conflict of interest. If not their interest, then mine. If I were an atheist, school prayer is not something I would want for my children. However, it is something atheists have to deal with daily. They should not have to put up with Christian prayers any more than someone who is Buddhists, Muslim, etc.

Politics is bad enough without religious influence. If our politicians were as religious as they claim to be, they would not be doing the things we see them doing regularly. Politicians seem to become corrupt as soon as they win their election. They go through life taking and taking. Then, when they are exposed, their religion becomes a point of emphasis. As though God has made them aware of their misguided mistakes and we need to forgive them because deep down they are good God-fearing people.

During the last Presidential election, there were numerous people vying to become our new leader. They told us about their faith. They told us how their faith plays a vital part in their lives. This is fine, but I do not want their religion to play any part in my life. I do not believe in God the way they seem to do. Others do not believe in God at all. I do not want my politicians to make decisions that affect my life, in any way, based on their religion.

Durie Burns

Currently, a Mormon is running for the Republican Party nomination, and there are people saying they will not vote for him because of his religion. A person's religion, or lack thereof, should not help or hinder his or her chance to lead our country. His or her stand on the issues and his or her integrity should be the only deciding factors. If religion plays a role in how a politician makes his or her stand on the issues, we need to question his or her motives. Let us keep religion out of politics and war. It is wrong for both.

# Chapter 14 – Religion and Racism

***This topic is definitely something we need to address.*** For years, I have heard that Sunday morning is the most racist time in America. Sunday is the day most people go to church. In addition, it is the time when many people of all races pray to God separately. Yes, some churches have congregations made up of people of different races, but the majority are segregated.

When I was growing up, I knew there were no White people attending our church. If there were any, it was because one had married someone in our race. Many religions have people in it who frown upon people from other races attending their church. They actively discourage other races from attending.

It happened to a friend of mine. He and his family moved to the Buffalo, New York, and decided to attend a Catholic Church in the area where he lived. They purchased a home in a predominately-White suburb. He told me his family had been attending this church for several weeks, but he felt he needed to find another church because he and his family felt unwanted. He said they were the only Blacks attending this church and he felt the church followers did not want them there.

He asked me if I knew of a Catholic Church where people would accept them. I told him about the Catholic Church my wife had joined in the inner city. I had attended the inner-city church with my family and told him it had a mixed congregation but was predominately Black. The head priest was White and some of his associate priests were Black. My friend made the decision to attend this inner-city church just so he and his family would feel more wanted.

I want you to understand that I am well aware there are some churches who welcome people of all races. However, many do not. If you are a minister of a church who does not go out of his or her way to welcome people of different colors, faith, etc., then you and your followers are not true Men and Women of God. I say you are hypocrites.

There is no place for racism in God's faith. There is no Black religion, no White religion, no Hispanic religion, etc. No matter what your color or ethnic background, God does not discriminate, and neither should those of us who claim to be his disciples and/or religious followers. In essence, I am saying that, if you discriminate against any individual because of their race, religion, color, sex, etc., you are in violation of what God really wants.

# Chapter 15 – It's up to Us

***My doubt about the truth of the Bible really started to grow when I attended Johnson C. Smith University in Charlotte, North Carolina, on a football scholarship as a 17-year-old freshman.*** As part of my education process, I had to take a required religious course. I do not remember the professor's name, but I do remember our first day of class.

At some point, the professor made the statement that, if a book left doubt in your mind after reading it, then maybe you should question that book. Having grown up in the church, I did have my doubts previously about the Bible. I had attended Sunday school throughout my childhood and as such, had studied the Bible as my Sunday-school teachers and ministers taught it to me.

I have read portions of the Old Testament, but it became boring, and I really did not care for the violence that was committed there in the name of God. Therefore, I decided to read parts of the New Testament to see if it provided any revelations that I could hold onto. After reading some of the New Testament, I am convinced, now more than ever, that God would not want the world to be in the turmoil we are in today.

I believe my doubts about the Bible and my becoming an investigator had something to do with my writing this book. I do not think someone who is enamored of the Bible could do it. They would not think about the Bible and religion the way I do based on investigative training, nor would they even begin to question its validity. In order to see something differently from the masses, you have to be able to step out of the box. You cannot step out of the box if you refuse to listen to another potential version of the truth.

I believe God is very upset with what is going on in this world and wants someone to do something about it. I do not know exactly what we can do. However, I do believe that God wants us to stop committing atrocities in his name. God does not want you to kill for any reason.

I just cannot understand how a person of faith, who believes in God, can justify killing people for any reason. Those men and women who commit suicide bombings in the name of their God are definitely going against God's wishes and teachings. Unfortunately, as I stated earlier, they follow men, and men tend to sway God's teachings to fit their needs. It is funny that not one religious leader who espouses the use of suicide bombers, has actually committed suicide himself. For some reason, these

*What God Really Wants*

religious leaders are not interested in becoming martyrs for the cause, as they want their followers to be.

I believe God wants us to help those less fortunate than we are. God is concerned about those of us who make millions of dollars in his name and use the money for personal gain or power. All I see, especially in America, is greed. The greed is so blatant that our own government officials are stealing from us. It happens all the time, yet President Bush and his cronies kept telling us how God was the centerpiece of their lives.

How can a person build a multi-million dollar church? I read where one minister built a $45 million church complex with not-for- profit money. The question I ask is, "Why?" Jesus never built a church. He preached by the water, on the rocks, or any other place he could find. He did not take money from the people to whom he preached, nor did he build shrines of wealth. I say, take this $45 million, build a church for $1 million, and use the other $44 million to help those who are in need.

Any minister of God who is wealthy should never have anyone in his or her congregation in need. No one whom they serve should be on welfare or need other government assistance. As God's spokesperson, the minister should be obligated to ensure that his or her followers are healed and whole before making himself or herself whole.

Durie Burns

I have talked with a number of religious ministers who agree with what I just stated. I asked them why they allow these so-called Men of God to enrich themselves. They say they cannot do anything about it. I told them that they not only *can* do something about it, but as true Men of God, are *required* to do something about it.

True Men of God need to unite and rid the world of the "False Prophets" who preach the Bible and use it for their own personal enrichment. These false prophets tell you God wants you to prosper. Some say that by "prosper," God meant for you to be rich. However, the false prophet is the one who is prospering by getting rich off his or her followers.

God wants us all to prosper, not just those who preach. However, God's interpretation of what it means to prosper does not necessarily equate to "make money." Prosper is a relative term. It can mean many things. In God's case, I choose to believe he wants us to prosper by believing in him and doing for others. In doing so, your life will become happier, and, therefore, you will have prospered.

God does not want restrictions placed on his believers by man. In fact, God has already forgiven us all for our sins—those sins we have committed and those we will continue to commit throughout our lives. He gave us clemency from all our sins when his son, Jesus, gave his life for our sins. At

*What God Really Wants*

least that is what they told me in church. They told me Jesus died for our sins.

When men want something, they tend to bend the rules to get what they want. Something is telling me to tell you that what man wants is not always what God wants. Do not accept man's word as God's word without examining the man delivering the message. Many so-called "Men of God" suck money from their congregation and use it for their own gain.

If I recall correctly, when Jesus asked his disciples to follow him, he in essence told them to give up whatever they owned and follow him. According to the biblical story, Jesus chose twelve people to help him teach God's word to the flock. These men did so willingly. I cannot find anything in the Bible that indicates that they made money or should have made money off God's teaching.

In fact, most of the twelve gave up their careers and commitments to follow and teach. While I believe that a person teaching God's word should receive enough to live a comfortable life, no messenger of God should be living a millionaire's lifestyle.

If a Man of God is living a lavish lifestyle and the funds used for this lifestyle came from his preaching in God's name, then his flock should also live that same lifestyle. That is what God really wants. God intended that those he created should share in what he worked to produce.

According to the Bible, after creating the Heavens and the Earth, God felt there was something very important missing. God realized he needed to create someone to enjoy the beauty he created. In what might have been the start of end of the world, God created Man. Man has become the most dangerous animal ever to inhabit Earth. For man has what no other animal on Earth has. Man has intelligence beyond reason. Man can think for himself and do for himself.

Our only hope is that man begins to understand what he is doing to God's world. If you are a person of God, you must agree that God created the Earth and all that it produces. Only God has the right to destroy it, and he does not want to do that. My God is a forgiving God, not a vindictive God.

We can change the course the world is headed toward. However, we as a people must stand up and tell our leaders, both religious and governmental, that we want this change. We have to start getting them to share their wealth with those who are in need. It is not sufficient for our leaders to spend millions of dollars on war.

We must get them to stop wars and use the money that would otherwise be wasted on carnage to make life livable for the people they serve. God wants this. It is up to us. We can continue believing in God as separate religions or we can unite all religions. We do not have to change our belief but rather our emphasis within our own religion.

# Chapter 16 – Free Will

***God gave us free will.*** You do not know how many times in my lifetime I have heard that statement from God-fearing people. Yet every time something happens, these same people cry that it happened because of God's will. I watch athletes claiming they won a game or championship because of their belief in God.

I shudder at their misguided belief that they won because of something God did. God has nothing to do with whether you win a game or championship. God does not take sides. Every time you compete in an athletic event, there are participants on both sides who believe in God. How can anyone assume that God would allow you to win and allow another of his believers to lose? It just does not work that way.

With free will, God gave us the ability to make our own decisions. The decisions we make can affect what we become and those all around us. Therefore, it is up to us to use this free will for the good of all people in the world. We need to ensure that we do everything possible for God's children.

*What God Really Wants*

No matter what your religion, you need to believe that God does not care how you believe in him, just as long as you believe. He has no concern if you choose to believe in him by yourself at home or with a congregation at church.

Therefore, let us stop telling people they cannot get to Heaven unless they believe in a particular religion. Let us teach our children that God will be there for you, no matter what, as long as you believe. You can believe in any religion on this Earth and still have just as good a chance to get to Heaven as anyone else has. However, people need to realize that their relationship with God depends on their relationship with other people on this Earth as well.

If you want to get to Heaven, make sure you do as much as you can for your fellow man. It might not seem like much, but when you help someone, you save a life. That someone may in turn save another life. And so on. You do not have to do anything major to obtain God's blessings. Your blessings will come when you help others receive their blessings.

It can work if we all put our differences aside and work toward ensuring that we take care of all God's children and none of them suffers anymore. Once we as a people have accomplished this goal, the world and the people in it will be able to walk in God's light. Until then we are just floundering and easily led by men and women whose only goal is to ensure their own self-gratification.

Let me see if I can make the point as simple as possible. Your religion is as good as and no better than anyone else's religion. Do not criticize the way a person believes in God. As long as they believe, that is what counts. However, you should use the free will God gave you to make the right decisions about whom you will listen to when you hear God's word. Do not waste it listening to people telling you how you can prosper through money or war.

Someone once said that money is the root of evil. They say it cannot buy happiness. I do not know if they are right, but I see much evil in people with money. Though they may think they're happy, in God's eyes they will never be.

However, money can save millions of people from starving, from disease, from homelessness, etc. If you truly want to be happy, use your money as much as possible, for the good of everyone you can and I guarantee you will be happy and God will be more eager to pave your way to his domain.

In order for us to accomplish this, we must unite worldwide. We cannot save the world from extinction through independent individual efforts. It must be organized, extensive, and without reservation. We all know we can do more for others. We must not wait or hesitate any longer.

*What God Really Wants*

Start at the bottom and work your way to the top. You will find people in need at the bottom and at the top. Yes, there are rich people who need your help as well. They are lost and cannot find their way. A little love from true people of God can make a difference in their lives as well. Maybe they will eventually see the light and begin to do what God really wants.

# Chapter 17 – My Dream

*I decided to include this chapter because of the waste of money I have witnessed throughout my lifetime in America.* Previously, I mentioned I had a dream to help the homeless, especially displaced veterans who are in their situation because of their inability to obtain employment. My focus for this chapter is the wasteful spending on wars and elections by our government officials. In addition, the money wasted by the Catholic Church to settle child-abuse lawsuits. Since 2001, America has spent, depending on which source you read, anywhere from $1 trillion to $4 trillion on wars in Iraq, Afghanistan, and Pakistan.

Previously, I discussed the settlement of child-abuse cases by the Catholic Church. The three incidents I cited total $930 million in payments made to individuals based on the abuses. We all know that the Catholic Church has settled many more cases than just these three. I sometimes wonder how much money the Catholic Church has and why it doesn't use that money to help those in need. However, I will not dwell on that issue at this time.

*What God Really Wants*

As for the waste of money spent by our government and/or private citizens on elections, I cannot begin to fathom the amount. However, I can focus on one particular aspect of the presidential elections of 2008. If my recollection serves me right, they spent approximately $100 million on security alone for the Democratic and Republican conventions. I do not know about you, but that seems like an enormous waste of money to elect a President.

I could be wrong, but I believe we are the only country in the world that spends such enormous sums of money to elect politicians. Other democratic countries have systems that allow for elections at a much lower cost than ours. Why is that?

If I could just get access to $100 million, I believe I could realize the beginning of my dream. How many apartment complexes could we build with just this money alone? I recently heard that someone built an apartment complex for approximately $5 million. Based on that statistic alone, it appears we could build approximately 20 complexes.

Even if we could only build 10 complexes, it is conceivable that we could take a substantial number of homeless veterans off the streets and into housing. If we included the money spent above by the Catholic Church and on wars, we could, in my opinion, completely eliminate homelessness.

Durie Burns

My dream is not just to house the veterans, but to create opportunities for them to find employment. The idea is to employ the residents of the housing complex to perform the duties necessary to run it. We would first identify those veterans who already have the skills and training necessary to complete certain tasks, then train those veterans who need additional education or vocational training so that they could perform the other required jobs in the complex.

I believe there is enough money available to initiate action throughout this country to end our homeless problem, if we stop the current needless waste of money. Maybe I am an idealist or just plain crazy, but I believe, if given the opportunity, I, along with those of you who are willing to help, can make a difference in the lives of so many Americans who have sacrificed to keep us free. We owe them that. For I believe this is what God really wants.

## About the Author

Durie Burns is a retired Special Agent in Charge of the Internal Revenue Service, Criminal Investigation Field Office, in Buffalo, New York. Prior to his employment with the United States Government, he served four years in the Air Force as an Air Policeman and Dental Assistant in New York State and England, respectively, during the Viet Nam War. Upon returning home from England, he completed college and began his career in Government service. Since his retirement, Durie and his family have moved to Northeast Florida where he spends his time traveling, writing, and playing golf. He is an avid golfer.

www.ingramcontent.com/pod-product-compliance
Lightning Source LLC
Chambersburg PA
CBHW020016050426
42450CB00005B/503